LEARN TO DRAW... EVERYTHING!

Illustrated by Kerren Barbas Steckler

Designed by Heather Zschock

PETER PAUPER PRESS, INC.
Rye Brook, New York

For Andrew

My everything! –KBS

PETER PAUPER PRESS

In 1928, at the age of twenty-two, Peter Beilenson began printing books on a small press in the basement of his parents' home in Larchmont, New York. Peter—and later, his wife, Edna—sought to create fine books that sold at "prices even a pauper could afford."

Today, still family owned and operated, Peter Pauper Press continues to honor our founders' legacy of quality, value, and fun for big kids and small kids alike.

Illustrations copyright © 2023 Kerren Barbas Steckler
Designed by Heather Zschock

Copyright © 2023
Peter Pauper Press, Inc.
Manufactured for Peter Pauper Press, Inc.
3 International Drive
Rye Brook, NY 10573 USA

Published in the United Kingdom and Europe by
Peter Pauper Press, Inc. c/o White Pebble International
Units 2-3, Spring Business Park
Stanbridge Road
Havant, Hampshire PO9 2GJ, UK

Library of Congress Cataloging-in-Publication Data

Names: Steckler, Kerren Barbas, illustrator. | Zschock, Heather.
Title: Learn to draw...everything! / illustrated by Kerren Barbas Steckler
; designed by Heather Zschock.
Description: Rye Brook, New York : Peter Pauper Press, Inc., [2023] |
Series: Young artist series | Audience: Ages 6 to 13 | Audience: Grades
2-3 | Summary: "This children's how-to-draw book contains simple visual
tutorials for drawing over 200 things. The book is printed in full color
and features animals, people, common objects, fantasy art, and more. A
table of contents and running page heads make it easy to find particular
subjects and themes"-- Provided by publisher.
Identifiers: LCCN 2022050389 | ISBN 9781441340511 (trade paperback)
Subjects: LCSH: Drawing--Technique--Juvenile literature.
Classification: LCC NC655 .L43 2023 | DDC 741.2--dc23/eng/20221020
LC record available at https://lccn.loc.gov/2022050389

Contents

Hey, young artists!

Are you ready to learn how to draw over **200** awesome things?
It's easy and fun!
Just follow these steps:

First, choose a picture you want to draw. You can use the Table of Contents to find different kinds of drawings, or just flip through the pages until you see a drawing you like!

Next, get a pencil and a piece of paper.

Then, copy each step of the drawing, starting with step 1. The new lines in each step are shown in red.

Lastly, color in your drawing! Use crayons, colored pencils, washable markers, or something else. You can copy the colors in this book or choose cool new colors of your own. If you like, draw a whole scene.

You make the rules, because you're an **amazing artist!**

GET READY! GET SET! DRAW!

GOLDEN RETRIEVER PUPPY

1.

START by sketching these simple shapes.

2.

THEN, follow each new step in red.

3.

4.

ERASE the gray lines.

5.

6.

7.

8.

GOLDEN RETRIEVER

1.

START by sketching these simple shapes.

2.

THEN, follow each new step in red.

3.

4.

ERASE the gray lines.

5.

6.

1.

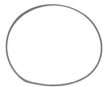

START by drawing the shape in **red**.

2.

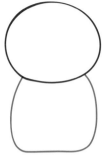

THEN, follow each new step.

3.

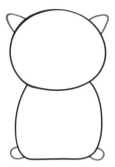

4.

5.

ERASE the gray lines.

6.

CAT

1.

START by sketching these simple shapes.

2.

THEN, follow each new step in **red**.

3.

4.

ERASE the gray lines.

5.

6.

SIAMESE CAT

1.

START by sketching
these simple shapes.

2.

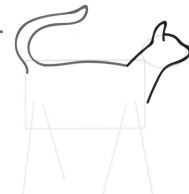

THEN, follow each new
step in red.

3.

4.

5.

ERASE the
gray lines.

6.

PERSIAN CAT

1.

START by sketching
these simple shapes.

2.

THEN, follow each
new step in red.

3.

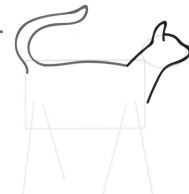

4.

ERASE the gray lines.

5.

6.

1.

2.

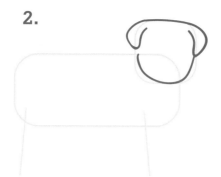

3.

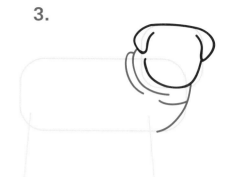

START by sketching these simple shapes.

THEN, follow each new step in red.

4.

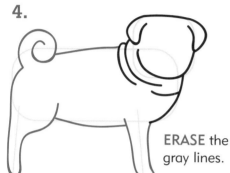

5.

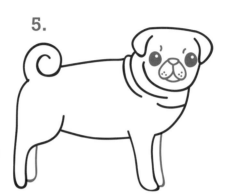

ERASE the gray lines.

6.

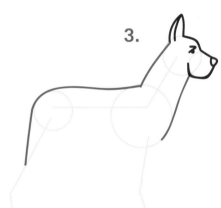

GREAT DANE

1.

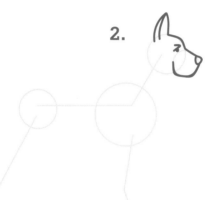

2.

3.

START by sketching these simple shapes.

THEN, follow each new step in red.

4.

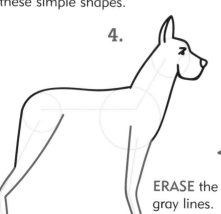

5.

ERASE the gray lines.

6.

8

1. START by sketching these simple shapes.

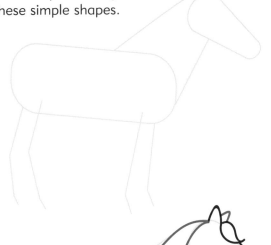

2. THEN, follow each new step in red.

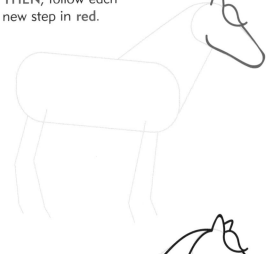

3.

4.

5.

6.

7.

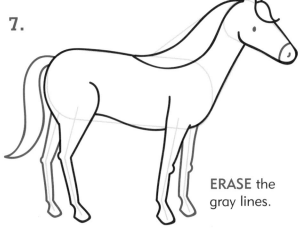

ERASE the gray lines.

8.

1.

START by drawing the shape in red.

2.

THEN, follow each new step.

3.

4.

5.

6.

ERASE the gray line.

CHICKEN

1.

START by sketching these simple shapes.

2.

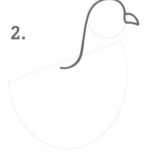

THEN, follow each new step in red.

3.

4.

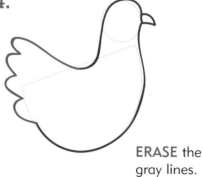

ERASE the gray lines.

5.

6.

GOAT

1.

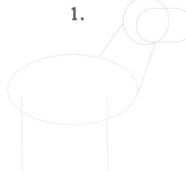

START by sketching these simple shapes.

2.

THEN, follow each new step in **red**.

3.

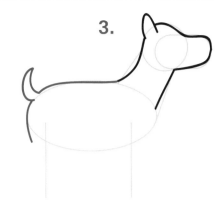

4.

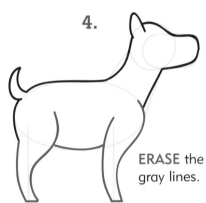

5.

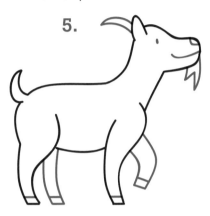

ERASE the gray lines.

6.

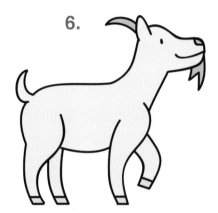

PIG

1.

START by sketching these simple shapes.

2.

THEN, follow each new step in **red**.

3.

4.

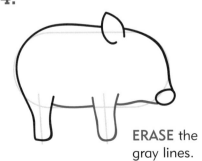

ERASE the gray lines.

5.

6.

11

1.

START by drawing
the shape in red.

2.

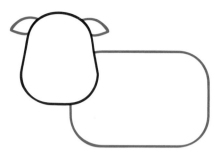

THEN, follow each
new step.

3.

4.

5.

6.

SHEEP

1.

START by drawing
the shape in red.

2.

THEN, follow each
new step.

3.

4.

5.

6.

1.

START by sketching this simple shape.

2.

THEN, follow each new step in red.

3.

4.

ERASE the gray lines.

5.

6.

7.

HUMMINGBIRD

1.

START by drawing the shape in red.

2.

THEN, follow each new step.

3.

4.

5.

6.

13

1.

START by drawing the shape in red.

2.

THEN, follow each new step.

3.

4.

5.

6.

7.

ERASE the gray lines.

8.

SEAGULL

1.

START by drawing the shape in red.

2.

THEN, follow each new step.

3.

4.

5.

6.

7.

8.

PIGEON

1.

START by drawing the shape in red.

2.

THEN, follow each new step.

3.

4.

5.

6.

7.

8.

ERASE the gray line.

9.

OWL

1.

START by drawing the shape in red.

2.
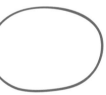
THEN, follow each new step.

3.

4.

5.

6.

7.

8.

1.

START by drawing
the shape in red.

2.

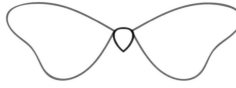

THEN, follow each
new step.

3.

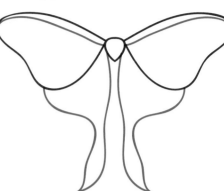

4.

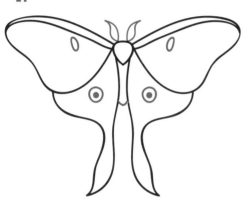

5.

6.

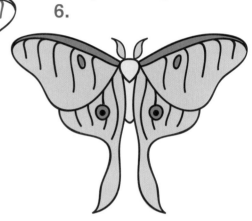

MONARCH BUTTERFLY

1.

START by drawing
the shape in red.

2.

THEN, follow each
new step.

3.

4.

5.

6.

7.

8.

BEE

1.

START by drawing the shape in **red**.

2.

THEN, follow each new step.

3.

4.

5.

6.

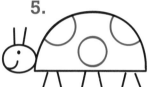

LADYBUG

1.

START by drawing the shape in **red**.

2.

THEN, follow each new step.

3.

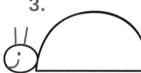

4.

5.

6.

DRAGONFLY

1.

START by drawing the shapes in **red**.

2.

THEN, follow each new step.

3.

4.

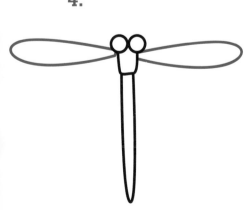

5.

6.

1.

START by drawing
the shape in **red**.

2.

THEN, follow each
new step.

3.

4.

ERASE the gray lines.

5.

6.

1.

START by drawing
the shape in **red**.

2.

THEN, follow each
new step.

3.

4.

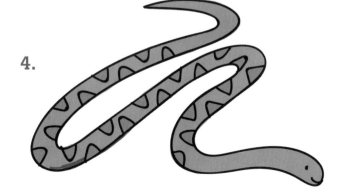

GECKO

1.

START by sketching these simple shapes.

2.

THEN, follow each new step in **red**.

3.

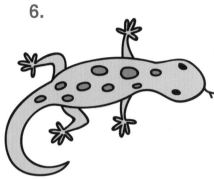

ERASE the gray lines.

4.

5.

6.

ALLIGATOR

1.

START by drawing the shape in **red**.

2.

THEN, follow each new step.

3.

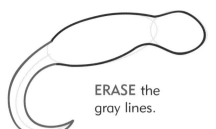

4.

5.

6.

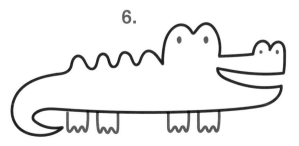

7.

1.

START by sketching these simple shapes.

2.

THEN, follow each new step in **red**.

3.

ADD antlers if your deer is a **stag**.

4.

5.

ERASE the gray lines.

6.

RACCOON

1.

START by drawing the shape in **red**.

2.

THEN, follow each new step.

3.

4.

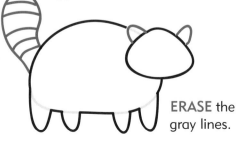

ERASE the gray lines.

5.

6.

BEAR

1.

START by drawing
the shape in **red**.

2.

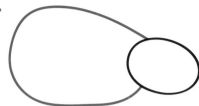

THEN, follow each
new step.

3.

4.

5.

6.

FOX

1.

START by drawing
the shape in **red**.

2. THEN, follow
each new step.

3.

4.

ERASE the
gray lines.

5.

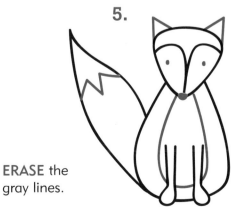

6.

21

1.

START by sketching
these simple shapes.

2.

THEN, follow each
new step in **red**.

3.

4.

ERASE the
gray lines.

5.

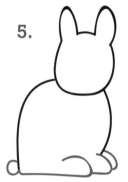

6.

7.

HEDGEHOG

1.

START by sketching
this simple shape.

2.

THEN, follow each
new step in **red**.

3.

ERASE the gray lines.

4.

5.

6.

MOUSE

1.

START by sketching
this simple shape.

2.

THEN, follow each
new step in **red**.

3.

4.

5.

6.

ERASE the
gray lines.

FROG

1.

START by sketching
these simple shapes.

2.

THEN, follow each
new step in **red**.

3.

4.

ERASE the
gray lines.

5.

6.

1.

START by drawing the shape in **red**.

2.

THEN, follow each new step.

3.

4.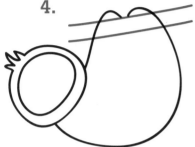

5.

6.

ERASE the gray lines.

CAPYBARA

1.

START by sketching these simple shapes.

2.

THEN, follow each new step in **red**.

3.

4.

ERASE the gray lines.

5.

6.

24

MONKEY

1.
START by drawing the shape in red.

2.
THEN, follow each new step.

3.

4.

5.

6.

7.

JAGUAR

1.

2.

3.

START by sketching these simple shapes.

THEN, follow each new step in red.

4.

5.
ERASE the gray lines.

6.

7.

1.

START by drawing the shape in **red**.

2.

THEN, follow each new step.

3.

4.

5.

6.

7.

8.

KANGAROO

1.

START by drawing the shape in **red**.

2.

THEN, follow each new step.

3.

4.

5.

6.

7.

GIRAFFE

1.

START by drawing the shape in red.

THEN, follow each new step.

2.

3.

4.

5.

ZEBRA

START by sketching these simple shapes.

1.

THEN, follow each new step in red.

2.

3.

4.

ERASE the gray lines.

5.

6.

7.

8.

27

1.

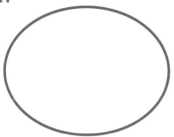

START by drawing
the shape in **red**.

2.

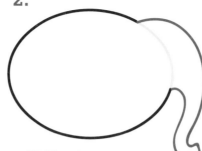

THEN, follow each
new step.

3.

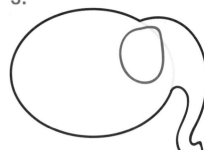

4.

ERASE the gray lines.

5.

6.

LION

1.

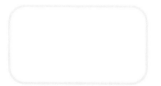

START by sketching
this simple shape.

2.

THEN, follow each
new step in **red**.

3.

4.

ERASE the gray lines.

5.

6.

HIPPO

1.

START by drawing the shape in red.

2.

THEN, follow each new step.

3.

4.

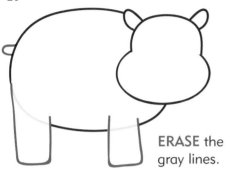

5.

ERASE the gray lines.

6.

MEERKAT

1.

2.

START by sketching these simple shapes.

3.

THEN, follow each new step in red.

4.

5.

ERASE the gray lines.

6.

7.

8.

9.

1.

START by drawing
the shape in red.

2.

THEN, follow each
new step.

3.

4.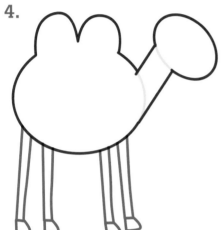

5.

ERASE the
gray lines.

6.

ARMADILLO

1.

START by drawing
the shape in red.

2.

THEN, follow each
new step.

3.

4.

5.

6.

PENGUIN

1.

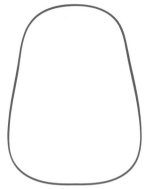

START by drawing the shape in **red**.

2.

THEN, follow each new step.

3.

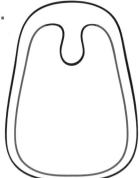

4.

5.

6.

SEAL

1.

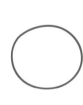

START by drawing the shape in **red**.

2.

THEN, follow each new step.

3.

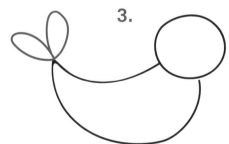

4.

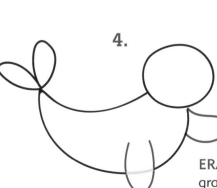

ERASE the gray line.

5.

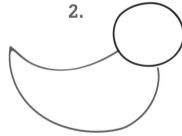

6.

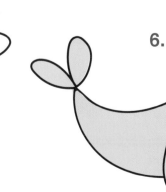

31

1.

START by drawing
the shape in red.

2.

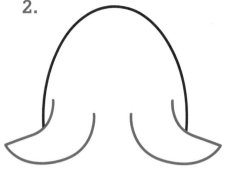

THEN, follow each
new step.

3.

4.

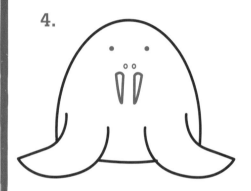

5.

6.

POLAR BEAR

1.

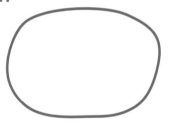

START by drawing
the shape in red.

2.

THEN, follow each
new step.

3.

4.

ERASE the
gray lines.

5.

6.

SHARK

1. START by drawing the shape in **red**.

2. THEN, follow each new step.

3.

4. ERASE the gray line.

5.

6.

HAMMERHEAD SHARK

1. START by drawing the shape in **red**.

2. THEN, follow each new step.

3. ERASE the gray line.

4.

5.

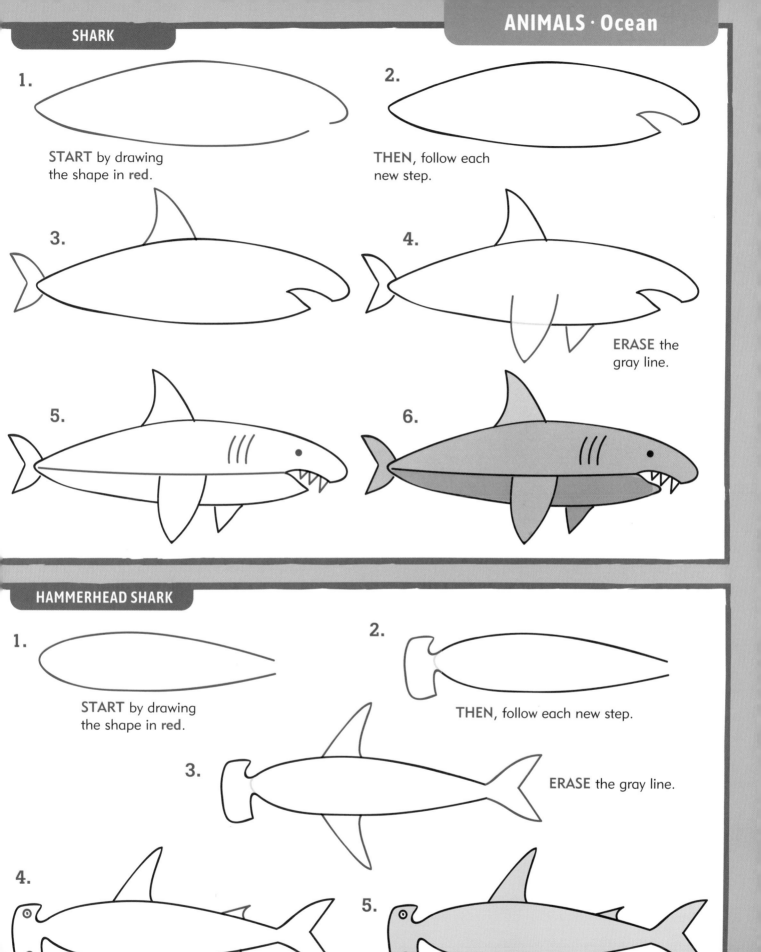

1.

START by drawing
the shape in red.

2.

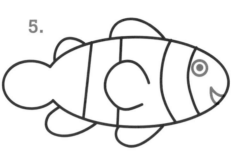

THEN, follow each
new step.

3.

5.

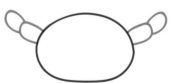

4.

6.

CRAB

1.

START by drawing
the shape in red.

2.

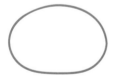

THEN, follow each
new step.

3.

4.

5.

6.

SCALLOP

1.  START by drawing the shape in red.

2.  THEN, follow each new step.

3.

4.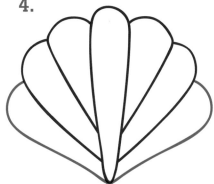

5.

6.

STARFISH

1.  START by drawing the shape in red.

2.  THEN, follow each new step.

3.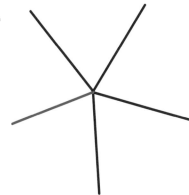

4.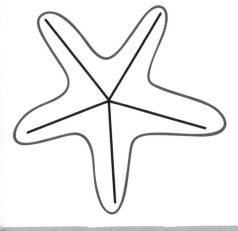

5.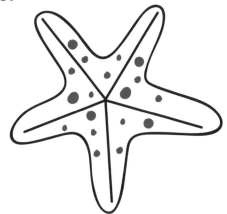

6.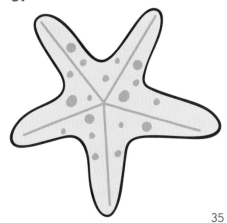

1.

START by drawing the shape in **red**.

2.

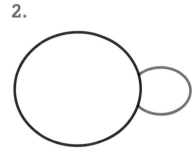

THEN, follow each new step.

3.

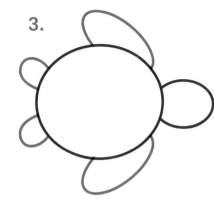

4.

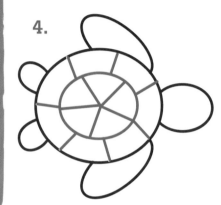

5.

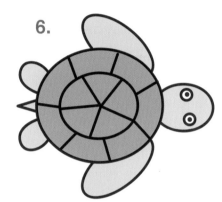

6.

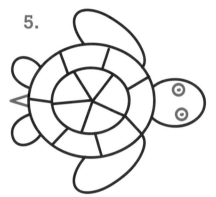

OTTER

1.

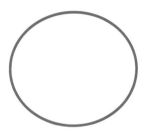

START by drawing the shape in **red**.

2.

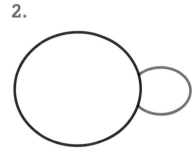

THEN, follow each new step.

3.

5.

ERASE the gray lines.

4.

6.

36

DOLPHIN

1.

START by drawing the shape in **red**.

2.

THEN, follow each new step.

3.

4.

5.

6.

BLUE WHALE

1. START by drawing the shape in **red**.

2. THEN, follow each new step.

3.

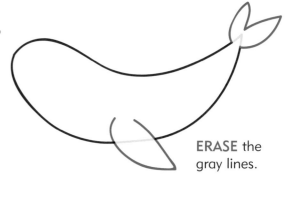

ERASE the gray lines.

4.

5.

1.

START by sketching these simple shapes.

2.

THEN, follow each new step in red.

3.

4.

5.

6.

7.

8.

9.

10.

11.

ERASE the gray lines.

12.

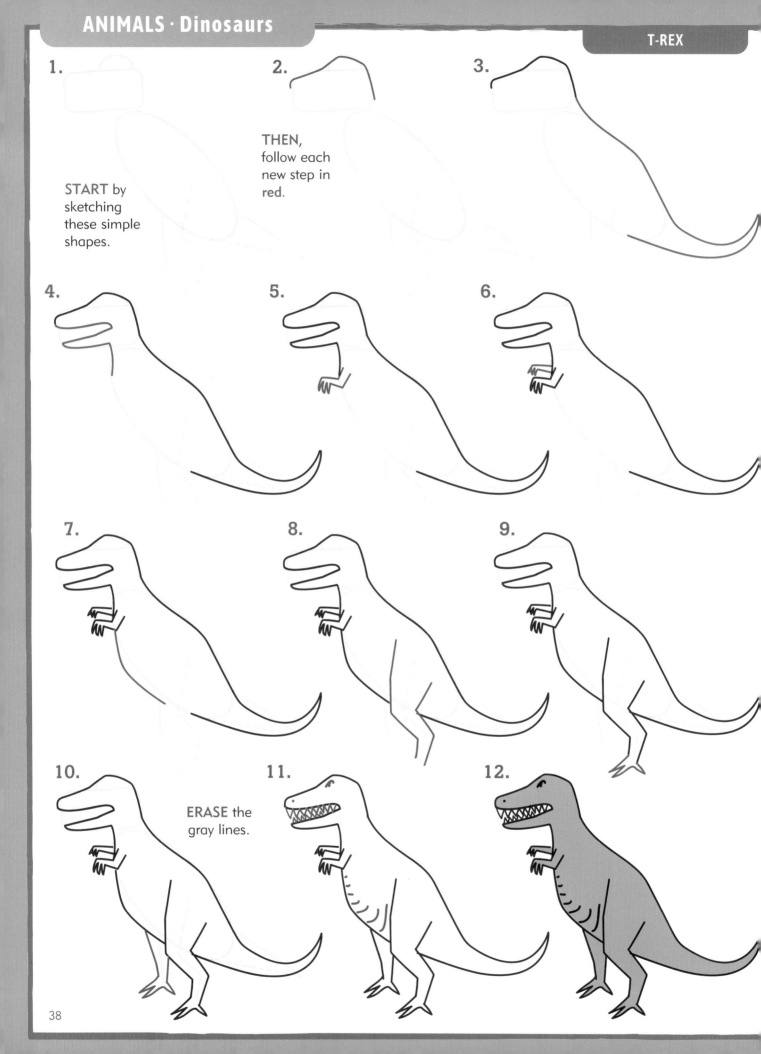

1.

START by sketching these simple shapes.

2.

THEN, follow each new step in red.

3.

4.

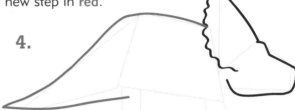

5.

6.

7.

8.

9.

ERASE the gray lines.

10.

11.

12.

39

1.

START by sketching these simple shapes.

2.

THEN, follow each new step in red.

3.

4.

5.

6.

ERASE the gray lines.

7.

8.

1. 2. 3. 4.

SIDE VIEW

1. 2. 3. 4.

SIDE VIEW

1. 2. 3. 4.

SIDE VIEW

1. 2. 3. 4.

SIDE VIEW

1. 2. 3. 4.

SIDE VIEW

41

PRACTICE drawing different emotions.

Try **DRAWING** all these different hairstyles.

1.

START by sketching
this simple shape.

2.

THEN, follow each
new step in **red**.

3.

4.

5.

ERASE the
gray lines.

6.

1.

START by sketching
this simple shape.

2.

THEN, follow each
new step in **red**.

3.

4.

ERASE the
gray lines.

5.

6.

BOY · FRONT

1.

START by sketching this simple shape.

2.

THEN, follow each new step in **red**.

3.

4.

5.

ERASE the gray lines.

6.

BOY · SIDE

1.

START by sketching this simple shape.

2.

THEN, follow each new step in **red**.

3.

4.

ERASE the gray lines.

5.

6.

1.

START by sketching this simple shape.

2.

THEN, follow each new step in **red**.

3.

4.

5.

ERASE the gray lines.

6.

WOMAN · SIDE

1.

START by sketching this simple shape.

2.

THEN, follow each new step in **red**.

3.

4.

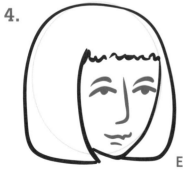

ERASE the gray lines.

5.

6.

MAN · FRONT

1.

START by sketching
this simple shape.

2.

THEN, follow each
new step in **red**.

3.

4.

ERASE the
gray lines.

5.

6.

MAN · SIDE

1.

START by sketching
this simple shape.

2.

THEN, follow each
new step in **red**.

3.

4.

ERASE the
gray lines.

5.

6.

47

1.

START by sketching
this simple shape.

2.

THEN, follow each
new step in **red**.

3.

4.

5.

ERASE the
gray lines.

6.

1.

START by sketching
this simple shape.

2.

THEN, follow each
new step in **red**.

3.

4.

ERASE the
gray lines.

5.

6.

STICK FIGURES are a great way to sketch out different poses. Here are a few to get you started.

1.

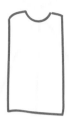

START by sketching
these simple shapes.

2.

THEN, follow each
new step in red.

3.

4.

5.

6.

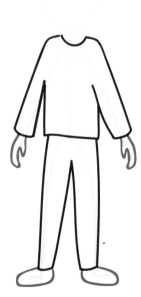

7.

ERASE the
gray lines.

8.

1.

START by sketching these simple shapes.

2.

3.

THEN, follow each new step in red.

4.

5.

6.

ERASE the gray lines.

7.

8.

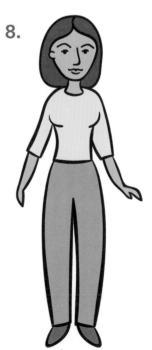

1.

2.

3.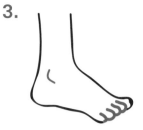

4.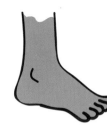

START by drawing the shape in **red** or lightly sketching simple shapes like below.

THEN, follow each new step.

1.

2.

3.

4.

5.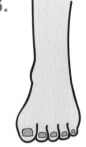

ERASE the gray lines as needed.

1.

2.

3.

4.

5.

6.

1.

2.

3.

4.

5.

1.

2.

3.

4.

5.

6.

1.
2.
3.
4.
5.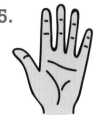

START by drawing the shape in red.

THEN, follow each new step.

1.
2.
3.
4.
5.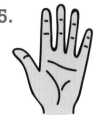

ERASE the gray lines as needed.

1.
2.
3.
4.
5.

1.
2.
3.
4.
5.

1.
2.
3.
4.
5.

1.
2.
3.
4.
5.
6.

1.

2.

3.

4.

START by sketching these simple shapes.

THEN, follow each new step in red.

5.

6.

7.

8.

ERASE the gray lines.

VARIATIONS

1.

2.

3.

4.

START by sketching these simple shapes.

THEN, follow each new step in red.

5.

6.

7.

8.

ERASE the gray lines.

VARIATIONS

1.

START by sketching these simple shapes.

2.

THEN, follow each new step in **red**.

3.

4.

5.

6.

ERASE the gray lines.

7.

8.

TODDLER

1.

START by sketching these simple shapes.

2.

THEN, follow each new step in **red**.

3.

4.

5.

6.

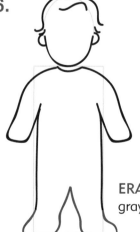

ERASE the gray lines.

7.

8.

TEACHER

1.

2.

THEN, follow each new step in red.

3.

START by sketching these simple shapes.

4.

5.

6.

7.

ERASE the gray lines.

8.

9.

1.

2.

3.

START by sketching
these simple shapes.

THEN, follow each
new step in red.

4.

5.

6.

7.

8.

ERASE the
gray lines.

9.

NURSE

1.

START by sketching these simple shapes.

2.

THEN, follow each new step in red.

3.

4.

5.

6.

ERASE the gray lines.

7.

8.

9.

1.

START by sketching these simple shapes.

2.

THEN, follow each new step in red.

3.

4.

5.

6.

7.

8.

ERASE the gray lines.

9.

1.

2.

3.

START by sketching
these simple shapes.

THEN, follow each
new step in red.

4.

5.

ERASE the
gray lines.

6.

7.

8.

9.

61

1.

2.

3.

START by sketching
these simple shapes.

THEN, follow each
new step in red.

4.

5.

6.

7.

8.

ERASE the
gray lines.

9.

1.

START by sketching these simple shapes.

2.

THEN, follow each new step in red.

3.

4.

5.

6.

7.

ERASE the gray lines.

8.

9.

1.

START by sketching
these simple shapes.

2.

THEN, follow each
new step in red.

3.

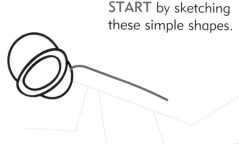

4.

5.

6.

ERASE the gray lines.

7.

8.

9.

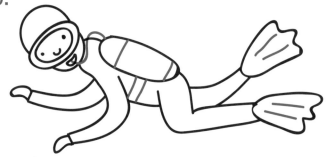

10.

2.

1.

START by sketching
these simple shapes.

THEN, follow each
new step in **red**.

3.

5.

4.

6.

8.

7.

ERASE the gray lines.

9.

T-SHIRT

1.

START by sketching the rectangle and then drawing the shape in red.

2.

3.

4.

THEN, follow each new step.

ERASE the gray lines.

SWEATSHIRT

1.

START by sketching these shapes and then drawing the shape in red.

2.

3.

4.

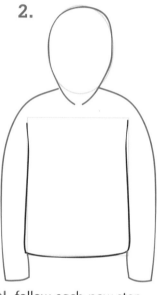

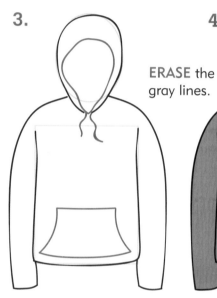

ERASE the gray lines.

THEN, follow each new step.

JEANS

1.

START by sketching the rectangle and then drawing the shape in red.

2.

3.

4.

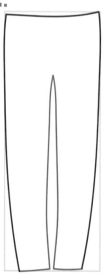

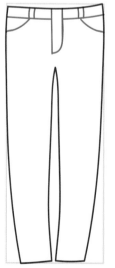

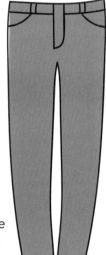

ERASE the gray lines.

THEN, follow each new step.

DRESS

1.

START by sketching these simple shapes.

2.

THEN, follow each new step in red.

3.

4.

ERASE the gray lines.

5.

COAT

1.

START by sketching these simple shapes and then drawing the shape in red.

THEN, follow each new step.

2.

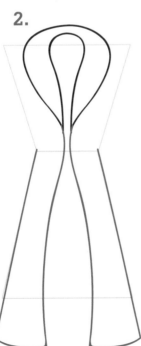

3.

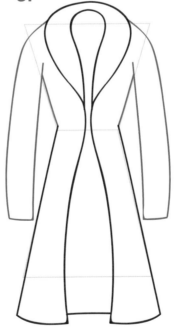

ERASE the gray lines.

4.

1.

START by sketching the shape in red.

2.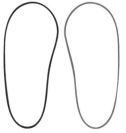

THEN, follow each new step.

3.

4.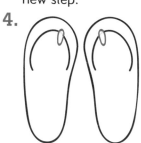

5.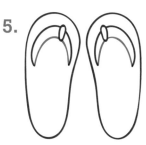

6.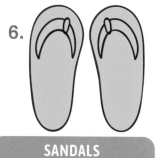

SANDALS

1.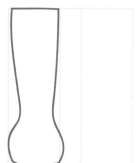

START by sketching these simple shapes and then drawing the shape in red.

2.

THEN, follow each new step.

3.

4.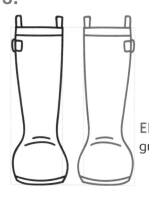

ERASE the gray lines.

SNEAKERS

1.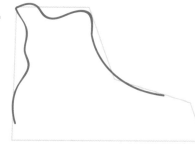

START by sketching this simple shape and then drawing the shape in red.

2.

THEN, follow each new step.

3.

ERASE the gray lines.

4.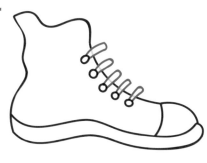

5.

6.

68

NOTEBOOK

1.

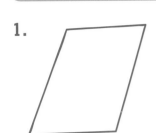

START by drawing the shape in red.

2.

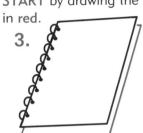

THEN, follow each new step.

3.

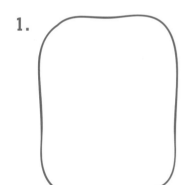

4.

5.

6.

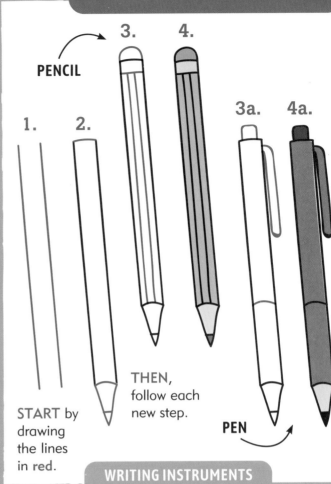

PENCIL

3. **4.**

1. **2.**

3a. **4a.**

START by drawing the lines in red.

THEN, follow each new step.

PEN

WRITING INSTRUMENTS

BACKPACK

1.

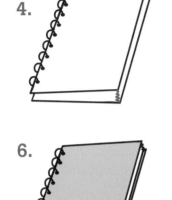

2.

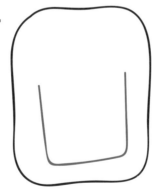

3.

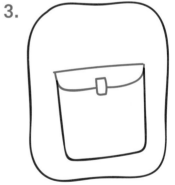

START by drawing the shape in red.

THEN, follow each new step.

4.

5.

6.

CHAIR

1.

START by drawing the shape in red.

2.

THEN, follow each new step.

3.

4.

5.

DESK

1.

START by sketching the square and then drawing the shape in red.

2.

THEN, follow each new step.

3.

4.

ERASE the gray lines.

5.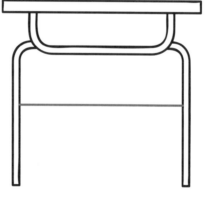

6.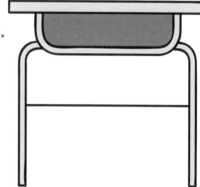

BOOK

1.

START by drawing the shape in red.

2.

THEN, follow each new step.

3.

4.

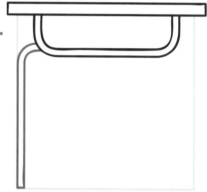

MICROPHONE

1.
START by drawing the shape in red.

2.
THEN, follow each new step.

3.

4.

5.

6.

7.

8.

GUITAR

1.
START by sketching these simple shapes.

THEN, follow each new step in red.

2.

3.
ERASE the gray lines.

4.

5.

6.

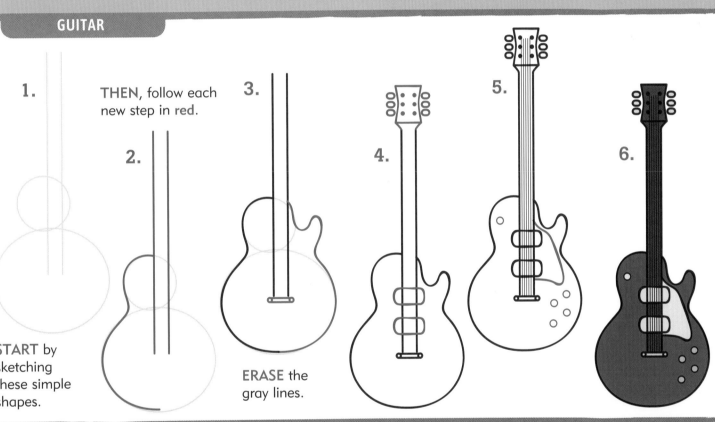

HEADPHONES

1.
START by sketching these simple shapes.

THEN, follow each new step in red.

2.

3.

4.
ERASE the gray lines.

5.

6.

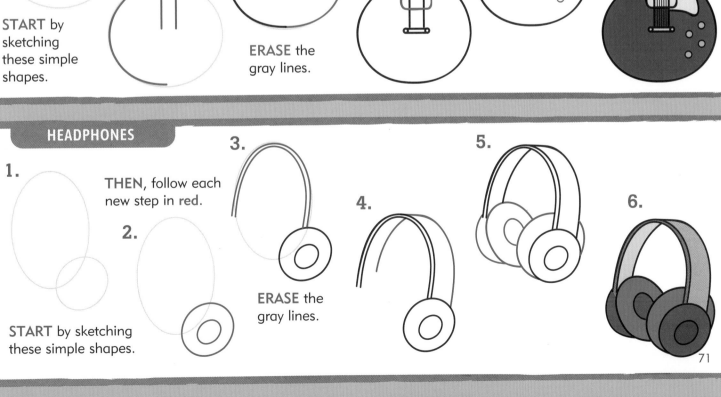

71

1.

START by sketching this simple shape.

2.

3.

4.

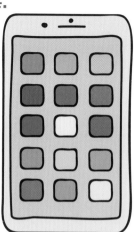

THEN, follow each new step in red. ERASE the gray lines.

LAPTOP

1.

START by drawing the shape in red.

2.

THEN, follow each new step in red.

3.

4.

5.

CAMERA

1.

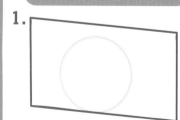

START by sketching the circle and then drawing the shape in red.

2.

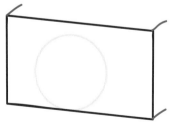

3.

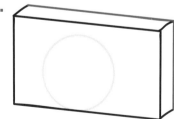

THEN, follow each new step.

4.

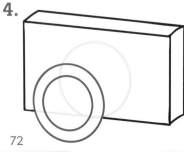

5.

ERASE the gray lines.

6.

BASEBALL

START by drawing the shape in **red**.

1.
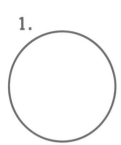

2.
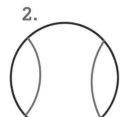

THEN, follow each new step.

3.
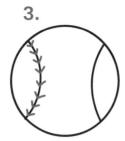

4.
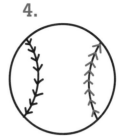

5.
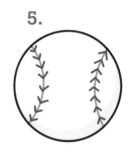

BASKETBALL

1.
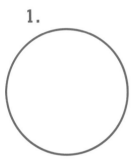

START by drawing the shape in **red**.

THEN, follow each new step.

2.
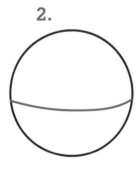

3.

4.

5.

FOOTBALL

1.

START by sketching this simple shape.

2.
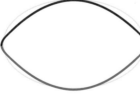

THEN, follow each new step in **red**.

3.

ERASE the gray lines.

4.
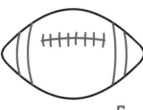

5.

73

BASEBALL BAT

1. START by sketching these simple shapes.

2. THEN, follow each new step in red.

3. ERASE the gray lines.

4.

5.

6.

BASKETBALL HOOP

1. START by drawing the shape in red.

2. THEN, follow each new step.

3.

4.

5.

6.

7.

8.

HOCKEY STICK/PUCK

START by drawing the lines in red.

THEN, follow each new step.

1.

2.

3. ERASE the gray line.

4.

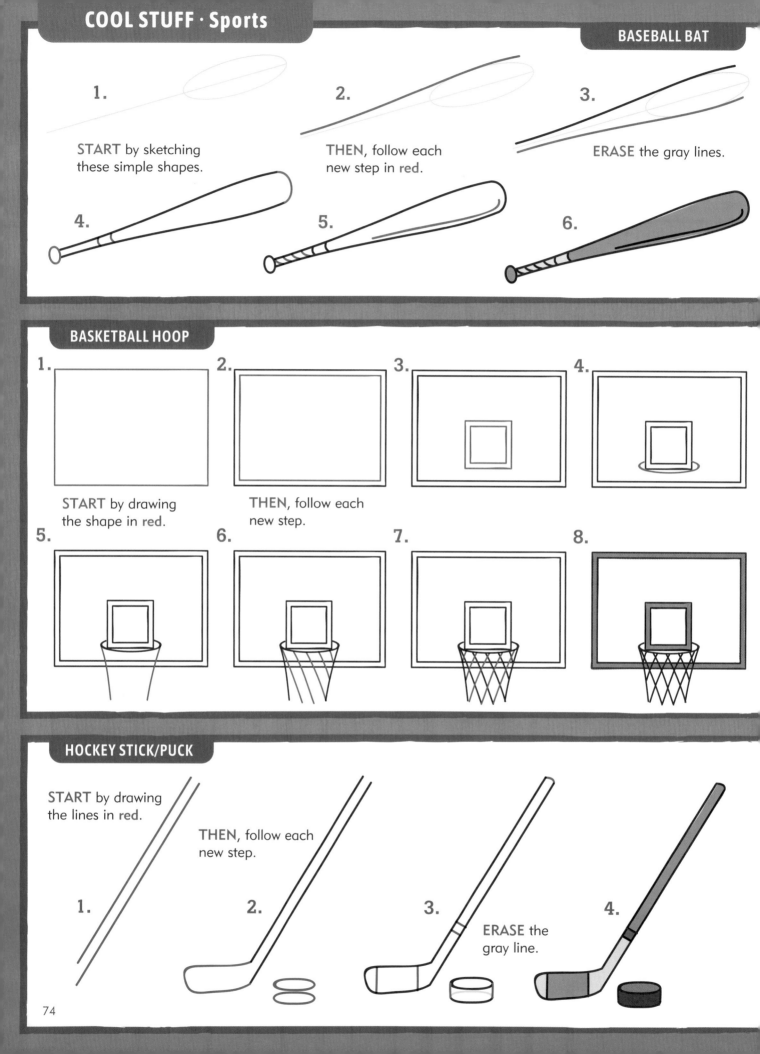

1.

START by sketching these simple shapes.

2.

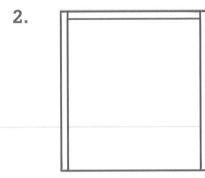

THEN, follow each new step in red.

3.

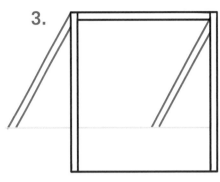

ERASE the gray lines.

4.

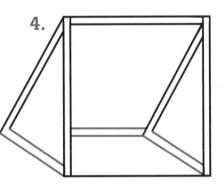

5.

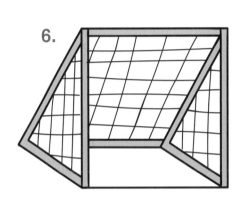

6.

ICE SKATE

START by sketching these simple shapes.

THEN, follow each new step in red.

1.

2.

3.

4.

ERASE the gray lines.

5.

6.

1.

2.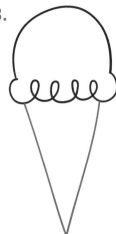

3.

4.

5.

START by drawing the shape in **red**.

THEN, follow each new step.

CUPCAKE WITH CHERRY

1.

2.

3.

4.

START by drawing the shape in **red**.

THEN, follow each new step.

ERASE the gray line.

5.

6.

7.

8.

POPSICLE

1.

2.

3.

4.

5.

START by drawing the shape in **red**.

THEN, follow each new step.

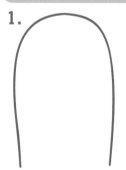 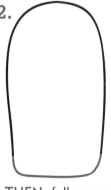 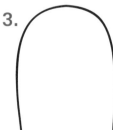 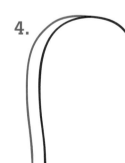 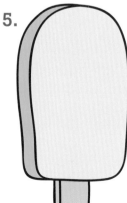

76

PIZZA

1.

START by drawing the shape in **red**.

2.

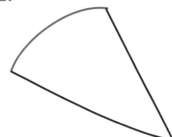

THEN, follow each new step.

3.

4.

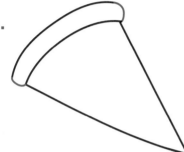

5.

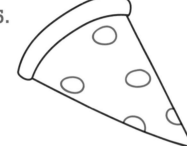

6.

SODA

1.

START by drawing the shape in **red**.

2.

THEN, follow each new step.

3.

4.

ERASE the gray line.

5.

6.

7.

8.

1.

START by drawing the shape in **red**.

2.

THEN, follow each new step.

3.

4.

5.

6.

STRAWBERRY

PINEAPPLE

1.

START by drawing the shape in **red**.

2.

THEN, follow each new step.

3.

4.

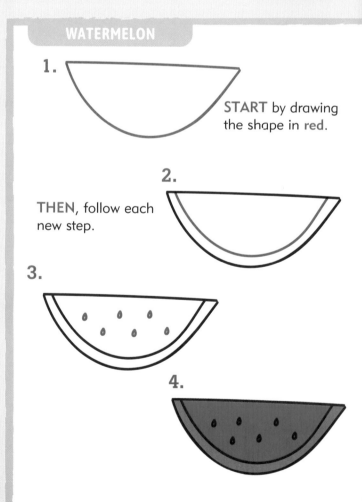

PEAR

1.

2.

START by sketching these simple shapes.

THEN, follow each new step in **red**.

ERASE the gray lines.

3.

4.

WATERMELON

1.

START by drawing the shape in **red**.

2.

THEN, follow each new step.

3.

4.

POPCORN

1.

START by drawing the shape in **red**.

2.

THEN, follow each new step.

3.

4.

5.

BURGER

1.

START by drawing the shape in **red**.

2.

THEN, follow each new step.

3.

4.

5.

6.

SLICE OF CAKE

1.

START by sketching these simple shapes.

2.

THEN, follow each new step in **red**.

3.

ERASE the gray lines.

4.

5.

6.

1. **2.** **3.** **4.** **5.**

START by drawing the shape in **red**.

THEN, follow each new step.

1. **2.** **3.** **4.** **5.**

START by drawing the shape in **red**.

THEN, follow each new step.

1. **2.** **3.** **4.**

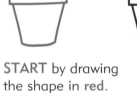   

START by drawing the shape in **red**.

THEN, follow each new step.

1. **2.** **3.** **4.** **5.**

START by sketching this simple shape.

THEN, follow each new step in **red**.

ERASE the gray lines.

80

DAISY

1.

2.

3.

4.

START by drawing the shape in red.

THEN, follow each new step.

ROSE

1.

START by drawing the shape in red.

2.

THEN, follow each new step.

3.

ERASE the gray line.

4.

5.

6.

1.

START by drawing the shape in **red**.

2.

THEN, follow each new step.

3.

4.

5.

SUNFLOWER

1.

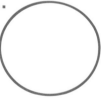

START by drawing the shape in **red**.

2.

THEN, follow each new step.

3.

4.

5.

SUN

1.

START by drawing
the shape in red.

3.

2.

THEN, follow each
new step.

4.

1.

START by drawing
the shape in red.

2.

THEN, follow each
new step.

3.

4.

CLOUD

RAINBOW

1.

START by drawing the shapes in red.

2.

THEN, follow each new step.

3.

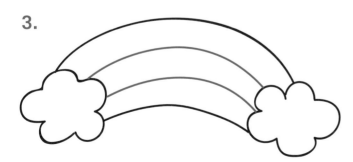

4.

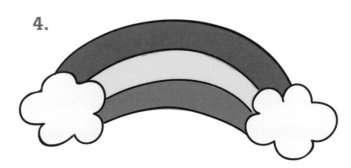

1.  START by sketching this shape.

2.  THEN, follow each new step in red.

3. 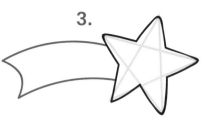 ERASE the gray lines.

4.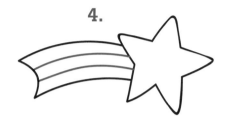

5.

MOON

1. 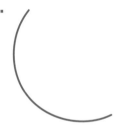 START by drawing the shape in red.

2. 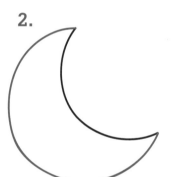 THEN, follow each new step.

3.

4.

PLANET

1. START by drawing the shape in red.

2. 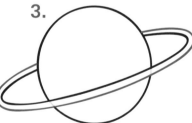 THEN, follow each new step.

3. ERASE the gray lines.

4.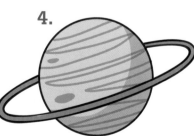

CAR

1.

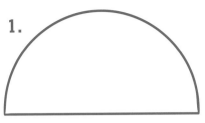

START by drawing
the shape in red.

2.

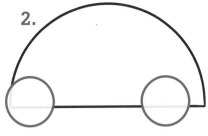

THEN, follow each
new step.

3.

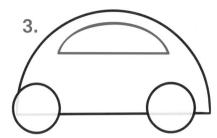

4.

ERASE the gray lines.

5.

6.

TRUCK

1.

START by drawing
the shape in red.

2.

THEN, follow each
new step.

3.

4.

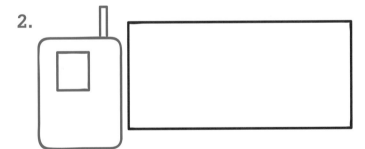

1.

START by drawing
the shapes in red.

2.

THEN, follow each
new step.

3.

4.

5.

6.

SCHOOL BUS

1.

START by drawing
the shape in red.

2.

THEN, follow each
new step.

3.

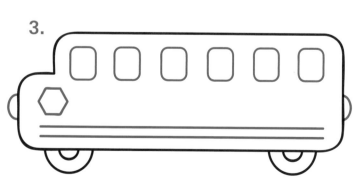

4.

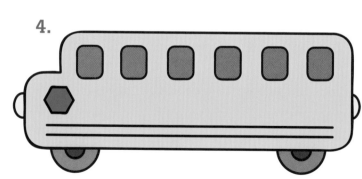

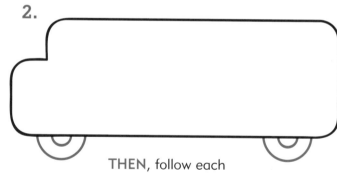

SUBMARINE

1.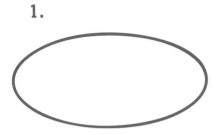

START by drawing the shape in red.

2. 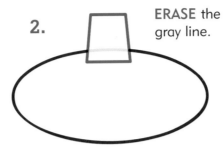 ERASE the gray line.

THEN, follow each new step.

3.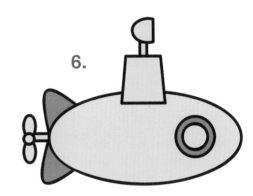

4.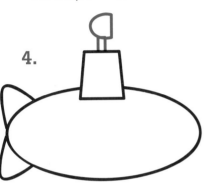

5.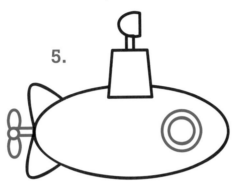

6.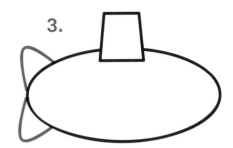

SHIP

1.

START by drawing the shape in red.

2.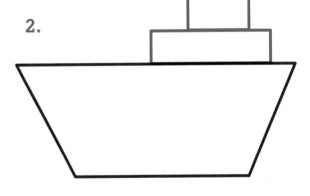

THEN, follow each new step.

3.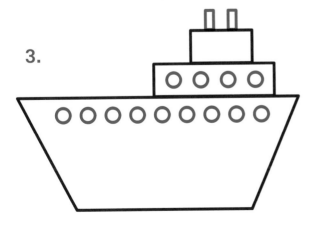

4.

1.

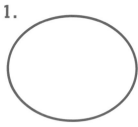

START by drawing the shape in red.

2.

THEN, follow each new step.

3.

4.

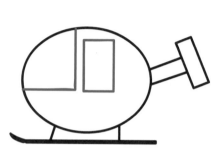

5.

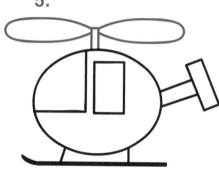

6.

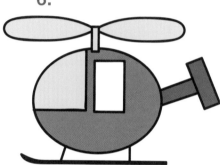

JET PLANE

1.

START by drawing the shape in red.

2.

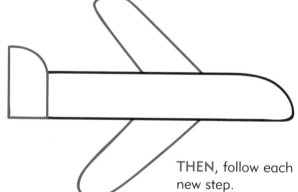

THEN, follow each new step.

3.

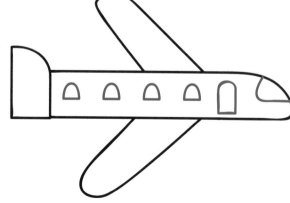

4.

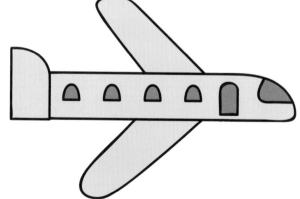

1.

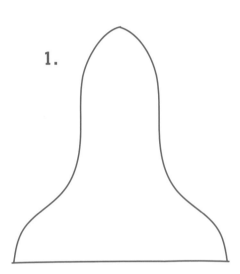

START by drawing the shape in red.

2.

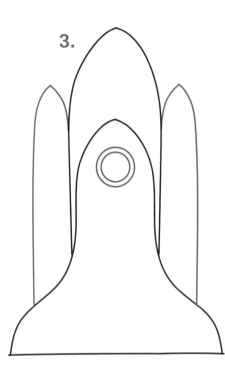

THEN, follow each new step.

3.

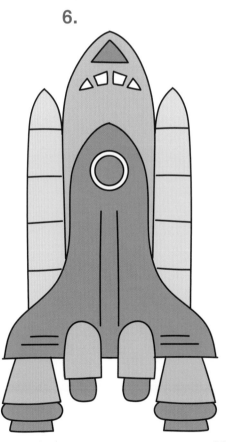

4.

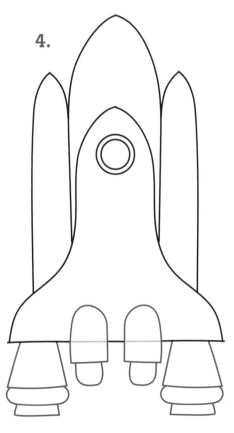

5.

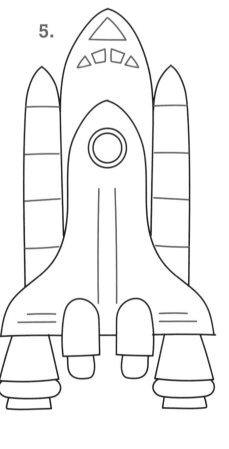

ERASE the gray lines.

6.

89

1.

START by drawing the shape in **red**.

2.

THEN, follow each new step.

3.

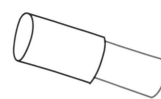

4.

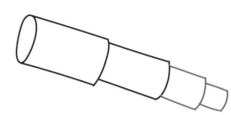

5.

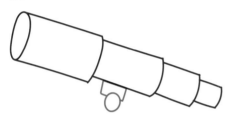

6.

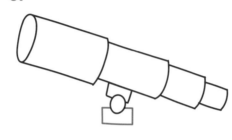

7.

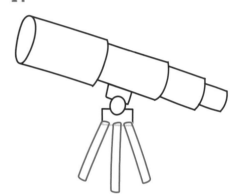

ERASE the gray lines.

8.

9.

10.

1.

START by drawing
the shape in red.

2.

THEN, follow each
new step.

3.

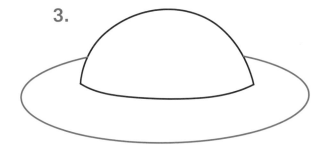

4.

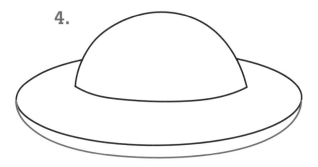

5.

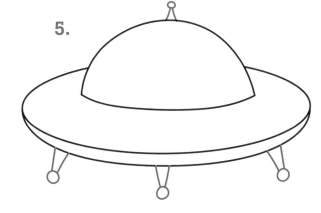

6.

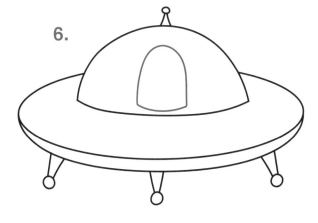

7.

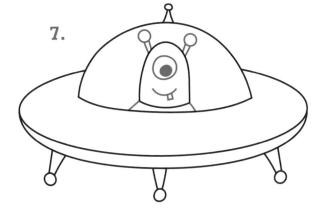

8.

1.

START by sketching these simple shapes.

2.

THEN, follow each new step in red.

3.

4.

5.

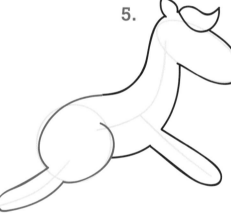

ERASE the gray lines.

6.

7.

8.

1.

2.

3.

THEN, follow each
new step in red.

START by sketching
these simple shapes.

4.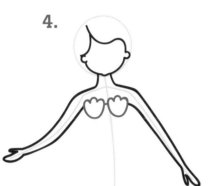

5.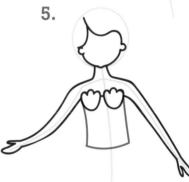

6.

7.

ERASE the
gray lines.

8.

1.

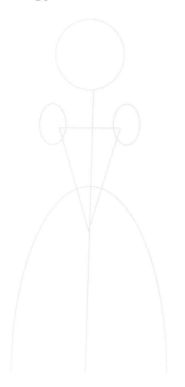

2.

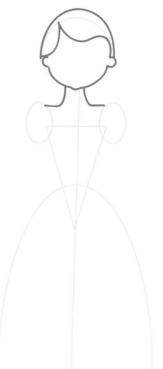

3.

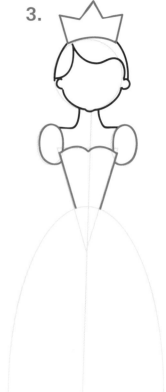

START by sketching these simple shapes.

THEN, follow each new step in **red**.

4.

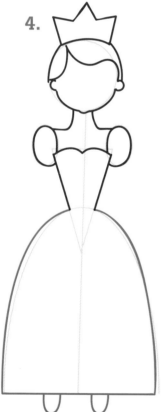

5.

ERASE the gray lines.

6.

1.

2.

3.

START by sketching these simple shapes.

THEN, follow each new step in red.

4.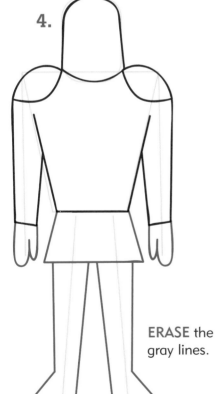

ERASE the gray lines.

5.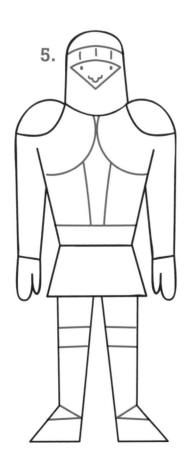

6.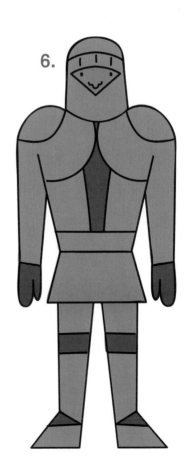

1.

START by sketching
these simple shapes.

2.

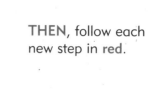

THEN, follow each
new step in red.

3.

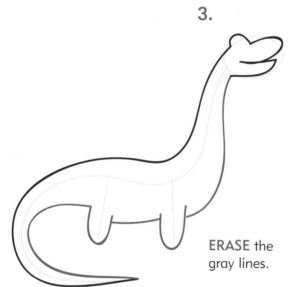

ERASE the
gray lines.

4.

5.

6.